WHO IS JESUS?

"Just like Meg Hunter-Kilmer, *Who Is Jesus?* is a faithful and captivating companion to scripture that encourages us to reflect on, wrestle with, and ultimately choose to love Jesus—especially in his living and effective Word. Both the novice and the scholar can fearlessly approach this Bible study and receive the Word of God, intelligent commentary, and gentle invitations to respond boldly to Christ's call to friendship. Keep *Who Is Jesus?* close and know that you are never alone on your journey with Jesus."

Chika Anyanwu
Catholic author and speaker

"Meg Hunter-Kilmer has given the Church a gift in these pages. With her trademark clarity, warmth, and love for scripture, she invites us not only to study the gospels but to encounter the living Christ within them. This book is not an abstract guide or a cold manual—it is a doorway into friendship with Jesus. Whether you are opening the Bible for the first time or returning to well-worn passages, you will find yourself surprised, challenged, and consoled by the God who speaks through every word. I cannot recommend this study highly enough for individuals, families, and parish groups who desire to fall more deeply in love with the Lord."

Fr. Patrick Mary Briscoe, OP
Host of the *Godsplaining* podcast and author of
Witness: A Guided Lenten Journal for Prayer and Meditation

"In this accessible Bible study, Meg Hunter-Kilmer does what she does best: She helps us enter the gospels in a way that leads not just to learning about Jesus but to meeting him face-to-face. In this study, she shares the kinds of questions that have borne fruit in her own decades of praying with the gospels. The result is a guide that breathes life into familiar stories and helps us encounter the God who loves us personally. Like a seasoned guide, Meg equips readers with just enough background to illuminate the text, clears away stumbling blocks, and then invites us into the scene with thoughtful questions that spark reflection and prayer. Whether you are new to scripture or have studied the Bible for years, you'll find yourself drawn deeper into the mysteries of Christ's life, death, and Resurrection—and closer to his heart."

Sarah Christmyer
Editor of the *Living the Word Catholic Women's Bible*
and author of *Becoming Women of the Word*

WHO IS JESUS?

DISCOVERING CHRIST IN THE GOSPELS

MEG HUNTER-KILMER

Ave Maria Press AVE Notre Dame, Indiana

Nihil Obstat: Reverend Monsignor Michael Heintz, PhD
Censor Librorum
Imprimatur: Most Reverend Kevin C. Rhoades
Bishop of Fort Wayne–South Bend
Given at Fort Wayne, Indiana, on September 22, 2025

The *Nihil Obstat* and *Imprimatur* are official declarations that a book or pamphlet is free of doctrinal or moral error. No implication is contained therein that those who have granted the *Nihil Obstat* or *Imprimatur* agree with its contents, opinions, or statements expressed.

Founded in 1865, Ave Maria Press is a ministry of the United States Province of Holy Cross.

www.avemariapress.com

Paperback: ISBN-13 978-1-64680-439-9

E-book: ISBN-13 978-1-64680-440-5

Cover and text design by Brianna Dombo Nicholson.

Printed and bound in the United States of America.

Library of Congress Cataloging-in-Publication Data is available.

CONTENTS

INTRODUCTION

When I first began reading the Bible, I was a thirteen-year-old fresh off my first retreat ever. "God wrote one book," I figured, "so I'd better read it."

So I started at Genesis and read through to Revelation and understood hardly a word. I made notes that I later had to cross out. I highlighted whole chapters for no discernible reason.

Even though I had no idea what I was doing, I have no regrets.

Oh, it would have been lovely to sit at the feet of somebody who knew scripture intimately and loved it deeply. But since that wasn't an option, I went with the next best choice: doing it badly.

Anything worth doing is worth doing badly, G. K. Chesterton tells us. And having read the Bible badly once, I went on to read it again less badly, and then more times less badly still. I gradually began to take margin notes that weren't wrong, and eventually notes that were truly moving.

And no matter how many times I read the Bible, there was always more to discover. Sometimes I'd find myself skimming a passage, assuming I'd found all there was to learn there, only to discover later that in fact I'd missed a thousand incredible connections. But for all I missed in my first blundering times through the Bible, I had understood its fundamental message: God's wild and unceasing love for us, which is the truth that every verse of scripture proclaims (if only we know how to read it).

Pope St. Gregory the Great tells us, "Scripture is like a river, broad and deep, shallow enough here for the lamb to go wading, but deep enough there for the elephant to swim." Each word and verse and passage carries the wisdom of God himself—a God so generous to his children that he speaks to us anew through his Word, whether we come to it for the first time or have given our lives to the study of scripture. Nobody is so learned that they have nothing more to discover, nor such a novice as to be unable to meet God in his Word.

This book is written primarily with the latter group in mind: If you haven't spent much time studying scripture, you're in the right place. Even if you're concerned that you might not be ready to take on a twelve-week Bible study—or any Bible study at all, for that matter—this book is for you. It will lead you through the highlights of the gospels, introducing you to the Jesus of scripture and inviting you to ponder his words, his miracles, his very person. It will sketch out the shape of his life, help you to draw connections to other biblical stories, and (most importantly) lead you into his Word, where you will meet the God who loves you desperately.

That said, "the word of God is living and effective, sharper than any two-edged sword" (Hebrews 4:12), and not even the Doctors of the Church could hope to look at a gospel story and feel confident that there was nothing more they could glean. Some readers may have read these stories dozens of times. Still, the Word of God is living and effective, and the more we open our Bibles, the more we'll find that God is constantly surprising us with passages we thought we knew backward and forward—especially when we come to them in a group and benefit from the wisdom of those we study alongside. Though you may be very familiar with the gospel passages discussed in this book, you will never exhaust their richness. If, on the other hand, you encounter a passage that you don't remember ever having heard before, you may find that this very freshness gives you a perspective that veteran scripture scholars would gain much from.

Each week, this study will present you with an assortment of gospel readings, along with some questions to ponder as you read. If possible, try to divide the readings up throughout the week, reading one passage in your Bible every day or two and responding to the questions in the space provided here. Using this book as a workbook will keep you accountable as well as help you to prepare for your Bible study meeting if you're working through this book with a group. The questions vary from the intellectual to the deeply personal, and each passage ends the same way: with an invitation to choose a word, phrase, or image to pray with. You may choose to memorize a line, or you may take ten minutes to sit with the words, slowly praying with them and letting the Spirit speak to your life. Whatever you do, don't let this Bible study be merely an intellectual endeavor that doesn't pierce your heart and transform your soul—the Word of God has more to offer than that.

If you do have the opportunity to gather with a small group to discuss these passages, you may (on occasion) find that you haven't had the chance to complete the reading when the meeting rolls around. Rather than staying home, trust that the Spirit will have something to say to you as your group reads the text together. Even if it takes you a while to collect your thoughts, and you find you have nothing much to contribute, there's great value in studying scripture in community and benefiting from others' insights.

The very best way to read the Bible is by reading the Bible—not a missalette or a Bible app or printouts of the readings, but your very own physical copy of a printed Bible, with all its footnotes and context and room for all your highlights and annotations. No Bible passage exists in a vacuum; we need to be able to study each one with a sense of what comes before and after, where it falls in salvation history, what scholars have come to understand about it, and how the Church reads it. And when you read not just *a* Bible but *your* Bible, and add your notes and markings and highlights, you'll find that you read more attentively, both the first time (when you're figuring out what to write) and each subsequent time (when you're drawn more deeply into the text and reminded of what God has done in your heart in the past).

Marking up your Bible also means that it becomes a precious gift showing how far you've come. The notes you make will be a record of all that the Lord has done in your heart over all the years that you've loved him. This book, too, may become a treasured keepsake, a resource you return to years from now to see just what the Lord was doing the first—or fortieth—time you really prayed with the annunciation or raising of Lazarus or walk to Emmaus.

Whether you're cracking the spine of your Bible and praying with scripture for the first time or carefully turning well-worn pages with notes scribbled in every blank space; whether you're sitting down with this book alone or gathering with a group of friends (or strangers); whether you're pondering scripture first thing each morning, grabbing five minutes at a time between piano and soccer practices, or poring over the gospel in the parking lot right before Bible study, this book will lead you into the Word—which will always lead you into the heart of Jesus.

A GUIDE FOR SMALL-GROUP LEADERS

This book can be used by individuals or by groups. If you feel called to gather a group and lead this study, you don't need to be a scripture expert—in fact, it may be easier if you aren't! Your job isn't to break open the Word for other people but to walk with them as you all dive into scripture together. As the leader, your role is simply to keep the conversation on track and help to move it along.

For many in your group, this may be their first time engaging in a Bible study; please encourage them to ask any questions or share any thoughts they may have. This is a safe space for them to work out any elements of the text that they find troubling—in fact, that's the first question after each reading. If the group raises a question you don't know the answer to, that's okay—this role isn't about giving answers. This endeavor is about encountering God's Word together, in all its strangeness. Your group may sometimes need extended periods of quiet as people look to the text again to see if anything else jumps out at them; there's no need to fill the silence.

Feel free to follow your instincts to lead this group. In general, it's best to start by reading the passage aloud, but some groups may choose to read it again silently before beginning to discuss. Ideally, participants will read the scriptures and jot down answers to the questions before coming to Bible study. Many will find it easier to participate if they prepare in this way, but others may find it more helpful to engage with the scriptures first as a group. Still others might prefer to prepare but find themselves unable to make consistent time to read in advance. Please encourage people to come as they are, whether they've prepared or not, and to make every effort at least to bring their Bibles and their Bible study books.

The questions in this book are a guide. While most people will benefit from reading the text thoughtfully and engaging with the questions here, they are offered here to prime the pump for a fruitful small-group discussion, not to direct the conversation. If your group reads a text and immediately begins a profound conversation, please ignore the questions and let the Spirit lead! You may even find that one single reading takes up the whole time—that's great! You could pick up where you left off the following week, or your group might decide to move on to the next chapter instead.

As with any small group, it's important to give every member the opportunity to share. That said, some of the questions in this book are quite personal. Nobody should feel pressured to divulge anything sensitive to the group. You may find it helpful to preface some questions with, "Obviously, there's no obligation to share, but did anybody have an example for question 4?" After pausing for people to nod, you might follow up by asking if anyone would like to share their story.

Understanding that some groups may have less to say, this study guide offers several readings each week to provide ample fodder for discussion. Most groups should find that ninety minutes gives enough time to get to all the readings, while those who meet for sixty minutes may need to choose what material to discuss. If you find that your group doesn't usually get to all the readings, you may open your discussion time by asking if there's a particular reading people want to start with. It's more important to have deep, meaningful conversations about the scriptures than it is to cover each passage. You are also welcome to take several weeks for each scheduled chapter and spend longer than twelve weeks on this study—whatever bears the most fruit for your group!

As you gather each week, you may find it helpful to build community by asking group members to share the highs and lows of their week. Of course, you'll want to begin and end each meeting with a prayer. As the leader, you may choose to open each meeting with an extemporaneous prayer and then invite participants to take turns closing the meeting with a prayer. Whatever approach you take, remember: Your job isn't to direct, to educate, or to convert. You're here to make space for the Spirit to speak. And the Spirit is used to working with all kinds of instruments. So place your group (and yourself) in the Lord's hands, and trust that it's all under control.

WEEK 1

INTRODUCTION TO BIBLE STUDY

Luke begins his gospel not with Jesus but with John the Baptist, with a story that parallels the account of Jesus's annunciation. Instead of Gabriel appearing to a peasant girl in a backwater town, Mary, he appears to Zechariah, a priest of God in the Temple—considered by the Jews to be the center of the world. As a priest, Zechariah was educated and respected, a man who was familiar with the things of God. Like most of the patriarchs, he and Elizabeth spent decades longing for a child. And so our gospel begins with a couple perfectly set up to be heroes. But when the angel came to answer the prayer Zechariah had prayed for decades, Zechariah's response leaves much to be desired.

After the story of Zechariah's doubt, Luke moves to a far less likely hero: a pauper in outlying Galilee—specifically Nazareth, of which St. Nathanael famously said, "Can anything good come from Nazareth?" (John 1:46). After Zechariah's monumental failure, the reader expects very little of young Mary. But her response to the angel was decidedly different, leaving us marveling at a story that reverses our expectations from the very beginning, one where the lowly are lifted up while the mighty stand by dumbfounded.

Before You Begin Reading

This may be your first time engaging in a Bible study, or it may be one of many Bible studies you've been part of. Take some time to reflect on your experience of Bible study in the past.

1. Have you read the Bible before? In what context (Bible study, personal prayer, religion/theology class, etc.)?

2. Do you feel comfortable discussing scripture? What makes you nervous or hesitant? What do you love about Bible study?

3. Tell us a little about the Bible you're using. Is it special to you? Is there a reason you use this translation? Have you highlighted it or taken notes in it? (It's okay if the answer to all of these questions is no.)

4. What are you hoping to get out of this Bible study? Why did you decide to study scripture in this way?

One important thing to note about Bible study is that you are welcome to ask any questions or share any thoughts you have. This is a safe space for you to work out the elements of the text (or of your faith) that you find troubling—in fact, that will be the topic of the first question after each reading.

The Annunciation to Zechariah: Luke 1:5–25

The Archangel Gabriel brings incredible news to a suffering couple.

Things to Know

- Ancient Jewish culture often understood suffering as being a punishment from God (see John 9:1-2); this was particularly the case when it came to infertility, making an already painful experience a source of even greater shame.
- Gabriel was already known to Zechariah because of his appearance in the book of Daniel, when he appeared at the time of the evening sacrifice to speak of a coming messiah (Daniel 9:20–27).

- When Gabriel declared that John would drink no wine, he was declaring to Zechariah that John would be dedicated to God, but also implying that he would be a great leader among his people, like Samson (Judges 13:4–7) and Samuel (1 Samuel 1:11).

Questions as You Read

This reading tells the story of the angel Gabriel's appearance to Zechariah, six months before Gabriel appeared in Nazareth with the good news of the Incarnation, the coming of God the Son into our world. Zechariah was a priest offering worship to God in the Temple when suddenly his long-unanswered prayer was answered in dramatic fashion—but his reaction isn't what we'd expect from a righteous biblical character.

1. What elements of this reading do you find moving? What elements do you find troubling? Confusing? Interesting?

2. Have you ever had a prayer go unanswered for months or even years? Were you able to keep praying for it? What did it feel like to carry that request for so long?

3. Why do you think Zechariah reacted the way he did? Does this remind you of anything similar in your own life?

4. Read Genesis 15:7–21, in which Abraham doubts God (15:8) and God responds by making a covenant with him (15:18). Both Zechariah and Abraham are childless men who doubt the word of God about their futures. Why do you think God's response to Zechariah was so different from his response to Abraham?

PRAYING WITH THE WORD

What is one word, phrase, or image that spoke to you in your reading? Record it here, and return to it in prayer this week.

The Annunciation: Luke 1:26–38

Gabriel returns with the news of our salvation: God with us, who will be made flesh in Mary's womb.

Things to Know

- The phrase "full of grace" was originally written in Greek with much stronger language than what we hear in modern English; one possible translation is "you who have been completely grace-ized."
- Though Mary and Joseph were not yet living together, betrothal had the legal force of marriage in Jewish law, making Jesus legally the son of Joseph (and thus a descendant of David).
- Matthew understands the annunciation as being the fulfillment of Isaiah 7:14: "'The virgin shall be with child and bear a son, and they shall name him Emmanuel' (which means 'God is with us')" (Matthew 1:23).

Questions as You Read

This reading is the hinge point of human history, the moment when God became man in the womb of an impoverished girl in an unknown town in an outlying province of the Roman Empire. Rather than skim over the text that you've probably heard proclaimed at Mass many times, try to enter in, using your imagination to picture the scene and hear the tones of voice used by Mary and Gabriel.

1. What elements of this reading do you find moving? What elements do you find troubling? Confusing? Interesting?

2. This reading is likely familiar to you. As you read this time, what surprises you? Is there anything you never noticed before? Any unexpected language?

3. How do you imagine that Mary felt when the angel appeared to her? Look at each message Gabriel gave her; what would you imagine her reaction to have been to each revelation?

4. What is your understanding of the purpose of Jesus's Incarnation? What does the angel say about it?

5. What similarities and differences do you notice between these two different annunciations? Take particular note of the locations, the statuses of the ones receiving the angel's messages, and their responses.

6. Have you ever felt that God was asking something particular of you? Were you able to say yes?

PRAYING WITH THE WORD

What is one word, phrase, or image that spoke to you in your reading? Record it here, and return to it in prayer this week.

WEEK 2

THE INFANCY NARRATIVES

As a rule, ancient biographies didn't start with the subject's infancy. They skipped unremarkable genealogies and parents' professions and childhood attributes and began the story when the subject rose to prominence. For Matthew and Luke, such an omission was unthinkable. And while we might long for far more stories about the young Jesus, the handful we're given are a treasure trove of information. As you read, turn your mind to what these stories tell us about the purpose of Jesus's Incarnation. God was made man to save us—why would his mother's visit to Elizabeth matter to us? What does the story of the inn and the barn tell us about God's unceasing love? What about the star and the wise men?

This week, we'll study a few key scenes from Mary's pregnancy and Jesus's infancy. Try to read slowly and attentively, allowing the Word of God to reveal the Lord to you in new ways, even through familiar texts. What is featured on Christmas cards but isn't in the text? What language is different from what you remembered? What details stand out? Allow the Spirit to speak to you through these small things.

The Visitation: Luke 1:39–56

Mary visits her cousin Elizabeth,
who has also found herself pregnant in a miraculous way.

Things to Know

- Luke uses language throughout this passage that depicts Mary as the new ark of the covenant (the vessel in the Old Testament that contained the presence of God)—see especially 2 Samuel 6.
- The phrase "blessed are you among women" echoes language used about two heroes of the Old Testament: Jael and Judith, both of whom destroyed the enemy of God's people by striking at his head.

- The prayer uttered by Mary here (the Magnificat) is prayed by every priest, deacon, and religious in the world (and many thousands of laypeople) every single evening.

Questions as You Read

After consenting to become the Mother of God, Mary hurried to see her cousin who was also unexpectedly expecting. As you read this passage, imagine yourself as one of the characters in the story. What strikes you most as you read?

1. What elements of this reading do you find moving? What elements do you find troubling? Confusing? Interesting?

2. Why do you think Mary chose to visit Elizabeth? Can you imagine other motivations as well?

3. Describe Mary as you've imagined her in the past and as she's been depicted to you.

4. Compare Luke 1:42 with Judges 5:24 and Judith 13:18 (words of praise about women who murdered enemy leaders). With this as a background to Elizabeth's proclamation, what else might Luke be telling us about the Blessed Mother? How does Genesis 3:15 shed light on this?

5. Mary's Magnificat is a stunning piece of poetry, inspired by the Holy Spirit and also by the poetic praise of another woman: Hannah, the mother of the prophet Samuel (1 Samuel 2:1–10). What similarities and differences do you notice between these texts? How do these two poems speak about God's heart for the lowly and oppressed? What might that indicate about our call?

PRAYING WITH THE WORD

What is one word, phrase, or image that spoke to you in your reading? Record it here, and return to it in prayer this week.

The Nativity: Luke 2:1–20

The God of the universe is born in a stable and laid in a feed trough, humbling himself for love of you.

Things to Know

- Jesus was born in Bethlehem, the hometown of the great King David (and the prophesied birthplace of the Messiah, as foretold in Micah 5:1).
- Though shepherds were generally looked down on in Jesus's culture, God chose to make them the first witnesses of the birth of Jesus, who is both the Lamb of God and the Good Shepherd who followed in the footsteps of so many heroic Old Testament shepherds.
- Verse 19 is the first of two times that Luke speaks of Mary pondering these things in her heart, offering her as a model of contemplation of the life of Jesus. (See Luke 2:51.)

Questions as You Read

There are few people in the Western world who aren't familiar with the story of the birth of Jesus. As you read it again, try to imagine the scene with fresh eyes to notice details you may have missed before.

1. What elements of this reading do you find moving? What elements do you find troubling? Confusing? Interesting?

2. What details stood out to you as you read the story this time?

3. What do the lowly circumstances of Jesus's birth tell us about who he is? What do they tell you about the call of Christians?

4. Discuss the angel's proclamation in verses 10–12. What do the titles the angel gives to Jesus communicate to you? What might they have communicated to the shepherds?

5. This story is full of juxtapositions of lowliness and glory. What might Luke's intention have been here? Does this resonate with your experience of life at all?

PRAYING WITH THE WORD

What is one word, phrase, or image that spoke to you in your reading? Record it here, and return to it in prayer this week.

The Epiphany: Matthew 2:1–12

Sages come bearing gifts for the Christ child.

Things to Know

- The Bible uses the word "magi" for the men often referred to as the "three wise men" or "three kings." This term comes from the Persian word for Zoroastrian priests and is used in the book of Daniel to refer to sages of Babylon as well. Though we can't be certain about their origin, it seems clear that they were seekers of truth who studied the stars to find wisdom and direction.
- King Herod the Great was an astonishingly rich (and shockingly violent) king who ruled over Judea. Not only was he not a descendant of David, he was, in fact, an Edomite—a kingdom against which the people of God had fought for many centuries.

Questions as You Read

Like the Nativity, the story of the "three" "kings" is one we feel we know well, though there are many things popularly depicted in Nativity scenes that aren't actually described in the Bible. Keep your eye out for the ways this story differs from the scene you imagine. Consider also the weight of emotions that many in the story may have felt, especially King Herod and those who feared him.

1. What elements of this reading do you find moving? What elements do you find troubling? Confusing? Interesting?

2. What did you discover wasn't actually included in the story that you'd always imagined?

3. Which character in this story do you find most striking? Which one do you identify most with?

4. In Matthew's gospel, the non-Jewish magi are the first to offer homage to Jesus. Why would this have been surprising to his Jewish readers? What does it communicate to us about the mission of Jesus? Consider Isaiah 60:1–16 and Psalm 72:1–14.

5. What have you heard about the meaning of gold, frankincense, and myrrh? Considering Exodus 30:23 and Song of Songs 3:6, what other symbolism might there be here? How can you offer similar gifts to the Christ child?

PRAYING WITH THE WORD

What is one word, phrase, or image that spoke to you in your reading? Record it here, and return to it in prayer this week.

WEEK 3

THE BEGINNING OF JESUS'S MINISTRY

We're told nearly nothing about the next thirty years of Jesus's life. But after those thirty years of being a son and a cousin and a neighbor and a friend, it was finally time for Jesus to reveal himself to the world as Messiah and Redeemer, Son of God and Son of Man. These opening moments of his public ministry are intentionally chosen to set the stage, to tell us who Jesus is and what he's here to do. He went to John to be baptized, at which point the Father cried out, "This is my beloved Son, with whom I am well pleased." After being buried with us in baptism, Jesus was tempted with us in the desert, where he engaged in battle with the devil—only a skirmish, but a foretaste of the victory he would win on Calvary. And then he worked his first public miracle—not a healing or a resurrection as one might expect, but an easing of a complicated social situation, a miraculous gift of joy.

Before he would become the wandering preacher and miracle-worker known so well to history, Jesus announced the world-changing work he came to do. As you read of these first movements of his public life, consider: How did Jesus want us to see him? Is this the Jesus you know?

The Baptism of Jesus: Matthew 3:13–17

Jesus is baptized in the River Jordan, and the Father declares Jesus his beloved Son.

Things to Know

- Ritual washing was an important part of the law of Moses; in the Old Testament it's used for cleansing from ritual impurity, but John's baptism indicated repentance and conversion of life.

- Mark tells us that "people of the whole Judean countryside and all the inhabitants of Jerusalem were going out to [John] and were being baptized by him in the Jordan River" (1:5). This crowd included pagans and sinners as well as the religious elite.
- Though John's prophetic voice (and popularity) made people wonder if he was the Messiah, he always insisted that he was as nothing compared to the one who was to come.

Questions as You Read

Jesus's first public action in all four gospels was to seek baptism from his cousin, John, who was baptizing in the River Jordan. John was offering a baptism of repentance, so he hesitated to baptize the sinless one, but Jesus insisted. When he was baptized, the Trinity began to reveal itself.

1. What elements of this reading do you find moving? What elements do you find troubling? Confusing? Interesting?

2. What is your understanding of the Sacrament of Baptism? How does this translate to Jesus's baptism?

3. Why might Jesus have chosen to inaugurate his public ministry in this way?

4. Meditate on the voice of the Father saying, "This is my beloved Son, with whom I am well pleased." Why do you think that's the message the Father gave in this moment? Can you imagine him saying this about you?

PRAYING WITH THE WORD

What is one word, phrase, or image that spoke to you in your reading? Record it here, and return to it in prayer this week.

The Temptation of Jesus: Matthew 4:1–11

Jesus resists Satan's efforts to tempt him to sin.

Things to Know

- Jesus's forty days in the desert echo Israel's forty years in the wilderness, but where Israel succumbed to one temptation after another, Jesus resisted.
- Each time Jesus responded to Satan, he quoted Deuteronomy, the book that tells of the end of the Israelites' forty years of wandering.
- Luke's account of the temptation ends by saying that the devil left Jesus "until an opportune time" (4:13, RSV2CE), pointing forward to the Passion, when Jesus would contend with the devil again.

Questions as You Read

Immediately after being baptized, Jesus was led (some translations say "thrust") into the desert where he fasted and prayed before beginning his public ministry. At the end of forty days, the devil appeared to him to tempt him.

1. What elements of this reading do you find moving? What elements do you find troubling? Confusing? Interesting?

2. What do you think the tempter was trying to accomplish here? What do you think he understood about Jesus that might be behind these efforts?

3. The devil quotes scripture here, but only selectively. In verse 6, he quotes Psalm 91:11–12. Look at that passage in the Psalms—what verse comes next? What might this teach us about the way we approach scripture?

4. The devil offered three temptations. What core temptation is at the root of each one (e.g., pride, sloth, pleasure, power, comfort, personal gain, etc.)? Which of these do you find most tempting in your life?

PRAYING WITH THE WORD

What is one word, phrase, or image that spoke to you in your reading? Record it here, and return to it in prayer this week.

The Wedding Feast at Cana: John 2:1–12

Jesus works his first public miracle at his mother's request.

Things to Know

- Jewish weddings in the first century were lavish affairs that went on for days; to run out of wine before the end of the celebration would have been a cause of great shame to both families.
- Rather than providing just enough wine for them to get by, Jesus gives them an absurd amount: 120 to 180 gallons, or close to a thousand bottles of wine. This image would have reminded John's readers of Old Testament passages that speak of the abundance of wine that would mark the age of the Messiah.
- John points out that this was the first of Jesus's signs (John's word for miracles), performed not just to protect the young couple but also to reveal his glory.

Questions as You Read

The first public miracle of Jesus wasn't a healing or a resurrection, but an easing of a tense social situation as Jesus offered joy and abundance where there had been scarcity. While reading, consider not only the meaning of this story to your life but also what it might have been like to be at a wedding with Jesus.

1. What elements of this reading do you find moving? What elements do you find troubling? Confusing? Interesting?

2. There's a peculiar exchange between Jesus and his mother in verses 3–5. What might John be trying to tell the reader through this conversation?

3. Why do you think Jesus chose to work this as his first public miracle? What was he trying to communicate?

4. Mary's intercession is very simple here—it is not a detailed explanation of the problem or a list of exact steps she expects Jesus to take to resolve it, but simply a trusting presentation about the people's need. What does intercessory prayer look like for you? How might you learn from Mary in this instance?

5. How do you imagine the scene at this wedding at Cana? Does Jesus dance? Laugh? Does he delight in offering this wine? Do you imagine God as being this joyful and generous, or have you perceived him as dour and stingy?

PRAYING WITH THE WORD

What is one word, phrase, or image that spoke to you in your reading? Record it here, and return to it in prayer this week.

WEEK 4

EARLY ENCOUNTERS WITH JESUS

The gospels are full of stories of people meeting Jesus and walking away entirely changed. Sometimes they experienced miraculous healing or earth-shattering mercy; other times, there was something subtler that changed their lives forever. Though not every gospel encounter with Jesus created a disciple, more often than not those who met Jesus in the pages of the Bible were drawn to him—whether they chose to follow him or not.

As you read these stories, ask yourself what it was about Jesus that prompted such intense devotion from those who met him. How do the evangelists describe him? Does that resonate with your experience of encountering Jesus? If not, why not?

The First Disciples: John 1:35–51

Immediately after his baptism, Jesus begins to collect followers who leave everything behind for him.

Things to Know

- Andrew and the other disciple (traditionally understood as John himself) were followers of John the Baptist, but after hearing his testimony about the identity of Jesus ("the lamb of God who takes away the sins of the world," "the Son of God"), they left their rabbi to follow Jesus.
- Nathanael speaks of Nazareth with disdain, despite himself being from Cana, a small village only about five miles from Nazareth that had nothing particular to recommend it.

- After Nathanael's abrupt about-face, he uses language that reminds the reader of the Davidic king, while Jesus's response hearkens all the way back to Jacob's ladder (Genesis 28:11–15).

Questions as You Read

John's gospel shows Jesus's first followers coming to him the day after his baptism. First we have Andrew and John, then Peter, Philip, and Nathanael in turn. Pay attention to what draws them to Jesus and what he says when he encounters them.

1. What elements of this reading do you find moving? What elements do you find troubling? Confusing? Interesting?

2. Andrew and John seem too shy to speak to Jesus, so he opens the conversation with his first spoken words in John's gospel: "What are you looking for?" It was a practical question, but also a meaningful one for each of us to ask of our presence in this Bible study, of our pursuit of Jesus, and of our lives. What are you looking for?

3. Jesus called Philip to follow, and immediately Philip went out and told Nathanael about Jesus. In your life, who has invited you into a relationship with Jesus? What did that look like? Have you acted as a Philip for someone else? Whom might Jesus be calling you to bring to him?

4. Look more deeply at Nathanael's story. How do you imagine Nathanael? Why do you think Jesus's statement that he saw

Nathanael under the fig tree prompts Nathanael to make such a profound proclamation of faith? Use your imagination to fill in the blanks of this conversation to make sense of Nathanael's abrupt reversal.

5. Which of these five men do you most identify with? Do you feel that you've met Jesus in some way? Do you feel that he's called you to come follow him? How have you responded?

PRAYING WITH THE WORD

What is one word, phrase, or image that spoke to you in your reading? Record it here, and return to it in prayer this week.

The Call of Peter: Luke 5:1–11

A miraculous catch of fish prompts Peter to leave his life behind and follow Jesus.

Things to Know

- The Lake of Gennesaret is also called the Sea of Galilee and the Sea of Tiberias, names that are all used in the gospels.
- On the Sea of Galilee, people fished at night; the fish were more active and closer to the surface, and the nets were harder for them to see. Asking a fisherman who had caught nothing all night to cast his nets again in the morning was like asking him to replace his tried-and-true bait with a leftover peanut butter sandwich.

- John tells a nearly identical story (John 21) but situates it *after* the Resurrection, when Peter, discouraged by his denial of Jesus, may have needed to be reminded that Jesus had chosen him on purpose.

Questions as You Read

Simon Peter had seen Jesus at work in the community (Luke 4:40–41). He had seen Jesus heal his mother-in-law (Luke 4:38–39). But still, he observed Jesus only at a distance until Jesus inserted himself into Peter's life.

1. What elements of this reading do you find moving? What elements do you find troubling? Confusing? Interesting?

2. Imagine how Peter felt at each stage in this story:
   a. After a long night of fruitless fishing.

   b. When Jesus asked him to row out and listen to him preach.

   c. When Jesus told him to cast his nets.

d. When the nets were filled to overflowing.

3. When you read about Peter elsewhere in the gospels, he doesn't seem like one who would ask for help. But here he called out to James and John for help, and those two went on to become some of Jesus's closest friends. What does this teach us about asking for help? Have you ever seen others benefit from your willingness to be weak?

4. We would expect Peter to fall at Jesus's feet and proclaim him Lord and God, but instead Peter asks Jesus to go away. Why? Can you sympathize?

5. Peter, Andrew, James, and John left everything to follow Jesus. What have you left behind? What might Jesus be calling you to leave?

PRAYING WITH THE WORD

What is one word, phrase, or image that spoke to you in your reading? Record it here, and return to it in prayer this week.

The Woman at the Well: John 4:4–42

A despised Samaritan woman becomes the first evangelist to the Samaritan people.

Things to Know

- Samaria was the capital of the northern kingdom of Israel, a country that had rebelled and formed their own nation, complete with their own half-pagan worship. Samaritans and Jews loathed each other.
- Generally, women went to draw water in the cool of the morning or the cool of the evening; if this woman was at the well in the middle of the day, it's likely that she was avoiding the other women of her community—and the complexity of her marital history may tell us why she might not have felt comfortable around them.
- Jesus doesn't tell us the circumstances of the woman's five marriages; though she may have been an adulteress, she may also have been widowed five times over, or five men may have walked out on her, or some mix of the above. The ambiguity can enrich our prayer.

Questions as You Read

Jesus went into Samaria, the home of the ancestral enemies of the Jews, and sought out a woman who was a social pariah. There he revealed to her the most direct claim to be the Messiah that he offered before his Passion (verse 26). The woman had been ostracized by her community, but having met Jesus, she now became an evangelist, bringing her former enemies to her newfound Lord.

1. What elements of this reading do you find moving? What elements do you find troubling? Confusing? Interesting?

2. Read verses 7–15 critically. We might find this language typical of Jesus, but he was a stranger to this woman (known to tradition as

St. Photina). Can you sense disdain in her voice? Shock? Imagine hearing these words from a disheveled stranger; how would you react?

3. Why do you think Photina asked to receive living water in verse 15? What can you imagine in Jesus's expression and tone of voice that might have drawn her?

4. Now imagine how she must have felt when Jesus brought up her marital status in verses 16–18. But though he knew all that about her, he still came looking for her. He still wanted her. What in your life has made it hard to feel that God might want you, might love you?

5. When Photina understood who Jesus was, she immediately went to tell everybody—even though they had spent years making her life miserable. Why?

PRAYING WITH THE WORD

What is one word, phrase, or image that spoke to you in your reading? Record it here, and return to it in prayer this week.

WEEK 5

JESUS'S TEACHINGS

The creeds we recite together emphasize the Incarnation of Jesus and also his Passion, Death, and Resurrection, but his life was about more than just his death. Jesus didn't come merely to die but to show us how to live, to lead us to the heart of the Father—not just by opening the gates of heaven, but by instructing us about what it looks like to follow him. The saints built their entire lives on studying the words and works of Jesus and trying to imitate him; while this study can only scratch the surface of Jesus's teachings, internalizing his teachings (highlighted in weeks 5, 9, and 10) is the work of a lifetime.

The Beatitudes: Matthew 5:1–12

Jesus flips the world upside down by praising the weak and the suffering and promising them God's kingdom.

Things to Know

- Matthew's Sermon on the Mount (chapters 5–7) is Jesus's longest series of teachings and forms the heart of his message. Luke and Mark recount different forms of this sermon, known as the Sermon on the Plain and the Sermon by the Sea, respectively.
- In going up the mountain, Jesus calls to mind Moses, who received the Ten Commandments at Mount Sinai. Jesus also evokes contemporary revolutionaries, who gathered crowds and gave speeches in the mountains, but who were calling for a very different type of revolution from the one demanded by the Beatitudes.
- The Church considers the Beatitudes a blueprint for holiness, reading them each year on the Solemnity of All Saints as a descriptor of those in heaven and an invitation to those on earth.

Questions as You Read

As he began his famous Sermon on the Mount, Jesus turned the world on its head. It's not the rich and the powerful and the comfortable who are blessed, he said, but the poor and the weak and those who are insulted and persecuted. This upside-down kingdom he inaugurated calls each of us to reevaluate our priorities and seek to conform our hearts to his.

1. What elements of this reading do you find moving? What elements do you find troubling? Confusing? Interesting?

2. Which beatitude do you find most comforting? Which do you find most challenging?

3. Considering these Beatitudes, what's an area of your life that needs to be reformed in order to fit into the upside-down kingdom of Jesus?

4. What's something concrete that you can work on this week to shape more of your life around the Beatitudes?

PRAYING WITH THE WORD

What is one word, phrase, or image that spoke to you in your reading? Record it here, and return to it in prayer this week.

Forgiveness: Matthew 5:38–48, Luke 17:3–4

Jesus demands of his followers a shocking degree of mercy in the face of the seemingly unforgivable.

Things to Know

- When Jesus says, "You have heard that it was said," his listeners would immediately have been on the defensive, as he was about to correct or deepen their conception of their religious laws as handed down from Moses.
- "An eye for an eye and a tooth for a tooth" is generally used in our world as a justification for retaliation. In its original context (Leviticus 24:19–20), however, it was intended not to permit revenge but to *limit* it, forbidding the injured party from demanding more suffering from the aggressor than was inflicted in the first place.
- Though in most translations Jesus calls on his followers to be "perfect" in Matthew 5:48, this word (*teleios*) is rather more complicated, expressing having attained one's purpose (that is, becoming completely Christ's). Parallel verses use different terms: "holy" in Leviticus 11:44 and "merciful" in Luke 6:36.

Questions as You Read

Throughout his public ministry, Jesus speaks of loving our enemies and forgiving those who hurt us. Bearing in mind that neither love nor forgiveness is a feeling, we read the hard words that he put into action when he cried out from the Cross, "Father, forgive them, they know not what they do" (Luke 23:34).

1. What elements of this reading do you find moving? What elements do you find troubling? Confusing? Interesting?

2. Jesus uses concrete examples here—examples that he himself offered us in his Passion. What connections do you see here between this passage in Matthew and the Passion of Jesus?

3. There are many things God asks of us that people find upsetting or off-putting: expectations about sexuality, about the time we give to the Lord, about our faith in impossible things, and about our willingness to love our enemies and forgive those who have hurt us. What do you find most challenging about following Jesus?

4. Does forgiveness always mean reconciliation? Describe a situation where you were called to forgive and also hold boundaries.

5. Is there anyone you need to forgive? How can you make a step in that direction this week?

PRAYING WITH THE WORD

What is one word, phrase, or image that spoke to you in your reading? Record it here, and return to it in prayer this week.

The Our Father: Matthew 6:9–15

When asked how to pray, Jesus gives his followers a prayer that encompasses all our needs.

Things to Know

- In Luke's version of the Our Father, the prayer is given to the disciples after they ask, "Lord, teach us to pray" (Luke 11:1).

- Nearly all translations say "daily bread" in verse 11, but the word translated as "daily" appears only twice in the Bible, both times in the Our Father as it appears in Matthew and in Luke; etymologically, "super-substantial" would be a more accurate translation, suggesting a link to the Eucharist.
- Though many Christian traditions finish this prayer with "for the kingdom, the power, and the glory are yours," that phrase is not found in the most ancient manuscripts or most early writings of the saints commenting on the Our Father.

Questions as You Read

When Jesus's followers asked him how to pray, he offered one prayer. Though there are many ways to pray, this prayer shows us what our posture toward God ought to be and challenges us to trust him more completely. Try to approach it with curiosity and intentionality rather than letting its familiarity wash over you.

1. What elements of this reading do you find moving? What elements do you find troubling? Confusing? Interesting?

2. How have you used this prayer in the past? How have you found it meaningful?

3. How did Jesus live out this prayer in his life?

4. Which line from the Our Father do you find most comforting? Which line do you find most convicting?

5. If you're being honest, which line is hardest for you to pray?

PRAYING WITH THE WORD

What is one word, phrase, or image that spoke to you in your reading? Record it here, and return to it in prayer this week.

Trust in God: Matthew 6:25–34

Jesus calls his followers to trust God in all things.

Things to Know

- Jesus was speaking to a group of people who were mostly living in poverty, so their concern about food and clothing was likely more about not being able to afford anything than it was about choosing between different options.
- Solomon was the richest of all the kings of Israel and the richest of all kings on earth during his reign (1 Kings 10:23); Jesus's allusion to Solomon's finery is intended to reassure his listeners by insisting that God can care for them even more abundantly than he cared for Solomon.
- Jesus uses the phrase "you of little faith" several times in Matthew, always to rebuke his followers for the anxiety they feel when they refuse to trust him completely (8:26; 14:31; 16:8).

Questions as You Read

Though the call to forgive and to love our enemies is among the most obviously challenging of Jesus's teachings, his invitation to trust God completely might be even more difficult. As you read this passage, consider the ways that you hedge your bets in life, making sure that you're taken care of rather than radically trusting God to provide for you.

1. What elements of this reading do you find moving? What elements do you find troubling? Confusing? Interesting?

2. Whether or not you struggle to afford food at this point in your life, in what areas do you find yourself anxious and worried?

3. Does Jesus's language here feel reassuring or dismissive?

4. Jesus says, "Do not worry about tomorrow; tomorrow will take care of itself. Today has trouble enough for today." Is it even possible to obey this command? What would it take to live with this kind of trust?

PRAYING WITH THE WORD

What is one word, phrase, or image that spoke to you in your reading? Record it here, and return to it in prayer this week.

WEEK 6

MIRACLES OVER NATURE

Jesus's ministry was marked by miracles, word of which brought people flocking to him by the thousands. He healed the sick, raised the dead, multiplied food, calmed storms, and walked on water. The gospels are so full of miraculous events that it's easy to gloss over them all. This week, we'll zero in on just three of Jesus's astonishing miracles that show his sovereignty over the created world.

In this section, we'll meditate on the power Jesus exercised then but also on the way that he satisfies our needs in large and small ways. As you read, ask the Lord for insight into moments when he has calmed the raging storms of your life, been miraculously present to you, or filled you when you were empty.

The Calming of the Storm: Mark 4:35–41

Jesus sleeps during a terrifying storm, then rises to calm the seas.

Things to Know

- The storm is so severe that Matthew's version describes it as a *seismos* or earthquake (Matthew 8:24).
- The image of Jesus asleep in the boat during the squall is reminiscent of Jonah sleeping through a storm (Jonah 1:5), though Jesus's sleep was rooted in calm whereas Jonah was hiding.
- Though several of Jesus's disciples were sailors and thus comfortable at sea, the Israelites in general were not a seafaring people. Their sacred literature demonstrates a conviction that only God can preserve those who find themselves in storms at sea (see Psalm 89:10; 65:8; 93:4; and 107:28–29).

Questions as You Read

This story is a curious one, showing Jesus leading his disciples into a storm and taking a nap in the stern of the boat while they fight for their lives. The juxtaposition of his calm and their panic is almost comical—and entirely familiar to most of us.

1. What elements of this reading do you find moving? What elements do you find troubling? Confusing? Interesting?

2. Do you think Jesus knew the storm was coming? Why did he lead the disciples into it? Why did he go to sleep and leave them to fend for themselves?

3. The disciples wake Jesus by crying, "Do you not care that we are perishing?" Does this cry of "do you not care" resonate with you? When have you felt abandoned by God?

4. Read Psalm 107:23–32 and Psalm 65:6–9. Given that the disciples would likely have known the Psalms quite well, what do you think their experience of the storm might have shown them? How does knowing God's power over the storms in your life change your reaction to them? How do you trust in him in the midst of chaos?

PRAYING WITH THE WORD

What is one word, phrase, or image that spoke to you in your reading? Record it here, and return to it in prayer this week.

The Feeding of the Five Thousand: Mark 6:32–44

Jesus feeds an enormous crowd with the lunch brought by one little boy.

Things to Know

- The feeding of the five thousand is the only miracle (other than the Resurrection) that appears in all four gospels.
- A similar miracle appears in Mark and Matthew, where Jesus feeds four thousand men (not counting women and children). Though some believe this is the same miracle recounted twice, the different details make it clear that Jesus did this on (at least) two separate occasions.
- The feeding of the five thousand hearkens back to the Old Testament, reminiscent of both the manna in the desert (Exodus 16) and Elijah's miraculous feeding of a hundred men with twenty loaves (2 Kings 4:42–44).

Questions as You Read

Jesus was moved with compassion for the people, who were like sheep without a shepherd, and so he worked a tremendous miracle—not just to show his power, but also to satisfy the needs of the people he loves.

1. What elements of this reading do you find moving? What elements do you find troubling? Confusing? Interesting?

2. What did Jesus first do in response to his understanding that the people were like sheep without a shepherd? How does his teaching the people parallel his feeding the people? What does his example say about our call to serve the lost and abandoned?

3. Why do you think Jesus begins by telling his disciples to feed the people themselves? What might his intention be in waiting to reveal his plan?

4. Matthew, Mark, and Luke say Jesus took the bread, blessed it, broke it, and gave it to the disciples, while John's gospel says he took the bread and "eucharisted" (gave thanks). Discuss the Eucharistic elements in this reading. How might this inform your experience of the Eucharist?

PRAYING WITH THE WORD

What is one word, phrase, or image that spoke to you in your reading? Record it here, and return to it in prayer this week.

The Walking on Water: Matthew 14:22–32

Jesus walks across the Sea of Galilee to be with his weary disciples.

Things to Know

- In Matthew, Mark, and John, the feeding of the five thousand is immediately followed by the walking on water—a bread miracle followed by a miracle in which Jesus's body is miraculously present where it had no business being. In John, these two miracles are followed by Jesus's proclamation that he is the Bread of Life, where he repeatedly commands his followers to eat his body and drink his blood (chapter 6).
- The fourth watch of the night took place between 3 and 6 a.m., indicating that the disciples had been battling the storm at sea for many hours. They got in the boat before it was evening and hadn't yet reached the other side.

- Mark's gospel says that Jesus "meant to pass by them" (6:48), which to our modern ears seems to indicate that Jesus was intending to walk past without stopping. But the language of "passing by" is used to indicate a theophany (a revelation of God) in the Old Testament, as in Exodus 34:6, 1 Kings 19:11, and Job 9:11.

Questions as You Read

Three gospels speak to us of Jesus's miraculous presence with his disciples following the feeding of the five thousand. But in Matthew's gospel, there's also a powerful encounter in which Peter steps out in strong-but-weak faith. Imagine the scene as you read.

1. What elements of this reading do you find moving? What elements do you find troubling? Confusing? Interesting?

2. Which disciple do you most identify with? Are you Peter, forcing your way out onto the sea? Are you another disciple, calling him back? Are you longing for the faith to join Peter? Are you judging him for falling?

3. Why do you think Peter was afraid? What is it that makes you take your eyes off Jesus and begin to sink into the chaos of your life? When you do start to sink, how do you cry out to Jesus as Peter did? Or do you have some other response to fear and failure?

PRAYING WITH THE WORD

What is one word, phrase, or image that spoke to you in your reading? Record it here, and return to it in prayer this week.

WEEK 7

LATER ENCOUNTERS WITH JESUS

The Christian life is first and foremost a matter of following Jesus. But while some people in the gospels left everything behind to follow Jesus, others transformed their lives radically without leaving home. This conversion could mean turning from grave sin, but it could also be a subtler transformation, an attitude of surrender or a decision to forgive. As you read these stories, consider how you are represented in the lives of these disparate followers of Jesus. What can you learn from their experiences?

The Sinful Woman Anoints Jesus: Luke 7:36–50

An unnamed woman washes Jesus's feet with her tears and anoints them with oil.

Things to Know

- Though modern Christians frequently use the term "Pharisee" to mean "hypocritical legalist," Pharisaism was a movement of deeply faithful Jews who sought to be unfailingly obedient to the law of Moses. As is often the case in religious renewal movements, many fell short of their ideals.
- Cultures in the Ancient Near East had strict and extravagant expectations for hospitality, not least of which was making it possible for guests to wash on arriving. Simon deliberately omitted these gestures of welcome.
- The woman's behavior went beyond the bounds of propriety, but Jesus commended her for her love rather than rebuking her for touching a man outside her family.

Questions as You Read

The gospels tell us of at least two distinct anointings that Jesus received from a woman: one just before his Passion (Mark 14:3–9) and the other here, by an unnamed woman in the home of Simon the Pharisee. Again, the familiarity of this image robs us of some of its meaning; it was no more common at the time of Jesus for a woman to rub her hair on the feet of a visiting religious leader than it would be now. Allow yourself to imagine the awkwardness of this scene and consider what that might teach you.

1. What elements of this reading do you find moving? What elements do you find troubling? Confusing? Interesting?

2. Consider the awkwardness of this moment for all concerned. Why might the woman have done such a thing? What uncomfortable situations might the Lord be calling you into?

3. Why does Simon condemn the woman? Whom do you dismiss as easily?

4. Jesus said, "Her many sins have been forgiven; *hence* she has shown great love." The parable helps to flesh out the meaning of

this unexpected saying: that she loves the more because of her sinful past. How can this be the case? Have you experienced something similar? What ugliness from your past has God thoroughly redeemed?

PRAYING WITH THE WORD

What is one word, phrase, or image that spoke to you in your reading? Record it here, and return to it in prayer this week.

Dinner at the Home of Mary and Martha: Luke 10:38–42

An overburdened woman calls out to Jesus for help.

Things to Know

- This is the first of three times we encounter Mary and Martha in the gospels. Later we'll see them mourning their brother Lazarus (John 11), then hosting a dinner at which Martha served and Mary anointed Jesus's feet (John 12).
- Sitting at the feet of a rabbi was an honor generally reserved for his disciples; Mary's presence at the feet of Jesus speaks volumes about his respect for women and his call for them to follow him as well.
- "Lord, do you not care?" is the same cry of despair that the disciples used when they were sure they were about to die in the storm at sea (Mark 4:38).

Questions as You Read

This passage is often used to condemn those who work to make things happen, as though Jesus were objecting to Martha's attentiveness to chores. Read the passage carefully, investigating your assumptions about what was asked of Martha and what she was corrected for.

1. What elements of this reading do you find moving? What elements do you find troubling? Confusing? Interesting?

2. Martha was burdened with much serving, which seems reasonable given all that is required to host a large group. Does this statement hit you differently if you consider that at this point in Luke's gospel Jesus had already fed the five thousand with five loaves and two fish (Luke 9:10–17)? What was it about Martha's serving that you think caused her to feel so anxious and burdened?

3. Martha was so frantic about her work that she became bitter toward her sister, resenting Mary for spending time with Jesus. She became so overwhelmed that even with Jesus right there with her, she cried out in despair. What might have led Martha to feel this way? Does any of this sound familiar to you?

4. Jesus's gentle correction of Martha is often depicted as being a harsh rebuke, leaving those who thrive on service (or who simply must fulfill the needs of their family or community) to feel that their work is meaningless or even detrimental to what is "really" important. But consider the context of this story: Immediately before going to Martha's house, Jesus insisted that service is essential for Christians (Luke 10:29–37). How does this context reshape

your understanding of his message to Martha? How might one find balance between work and prayer?

5. Many translations show Jesus chiding Martha for being anxious. Is this a condemnation of people with clinical anxiety? What does Jesus mean when he tells people not to worry? How is it possible to obey this command?

PRAYING WITH THE WORD

What is one word, phrase, or image that spoke to you in your reading? Record it here, and return to it in prayer this week.

The Encounter with Zacchaeus: Luke 19:1–10

A public sinner is so eager to see Jesus that he makes a fool of himself to do it.

Things to Know

- Tax collectors weren't merely bureaucrats but collaborators with the oppressive Roman overlords, men who betrayed their people in order to pad their bank accounts. Most of them became rich through extortion, demanding even more from their countrymen than the exorbitant taxes levied by Rome.

- It was considered undignified for grown men to run or to climb trees.
- The law of Moses required that thieves make restitution of what they'd stolen, restoring 120 percent to their victims (Numbers 5:7) or possibly 200 percent (Exodus 22:3). The best Old Testament foundation for restoring something fourfold (as Zacchaeus promised to do) is David's insistence that a theft that constituted a betrayal must be repaid fourfold (2 Samuel 12:6).

Questions as You Read

Lest we think that perhaps Zacchaeus was a secretly righteous tax collector, Luke elaborates: He was a wealthy man, feasting as his people starved. But there was something about Jesus that called to him, so much so that he forsook his dignity by running through the streets and climbing a tree to see the passing rabbi.

1. What elements of this reading do you find moving? What elements do you find troubling? Confusing? Interesting?

2. What kind of man must Jesus have been to appeal to one such as Zacchaeus? What must Zacchaeus have heard about Jesus that convinced him to risk everything not even for a conversation but merely for a glimpse?

3. Is this the Jesus you know? Compare this description of Jesus to the one you've heard preached, to the Jesus you've seen depicted in art and film.

4. The people must have ridiculed the pathetic little man for his desperation to see Jesus, but when Jesus loved this outcast and offered him forgiveness, he took Zacchaeus's shame upon himself. Discuss the crowd's response to Jesus and how it might foreshadow the Cross.

5. On scrambling down out of the tree, Zacchaeus immediately gave back 400 percent of what he had stolen, dismantling his idols from the moment he met Jesus. What idols in your life do you need to dismantle with God's help? What would it take for you to make a first step?

PRAYING WITH THE WORD

What is one word, phrase, or image that spoke to you in your reading? Record it here, and return to it in prayer this week.

WEEK 8

PARABLES

Though we tend to think of Jesus as teaching exclusively in parables, it wasn't until about halfway through his ministry that he began using these stories to teach his followers. These stories are revelatory not just because they're easy to remember but also because they invite us to meditate on layers of meaning and to consider an image from many different angles. While at times Jesus explains the meaning of a parable, even then the Spirit often has more to say to us through the imagery Jesus used.

Though parables often bear fruit in our lives because of the ways they reveal God's truth, Jesus made it clear that he used parables not because they were rich or memorable but actually because they were difficult for non-believers to understand (Matthew 13:10–13). For much of his ministry, he was concealing his identity and his plans from those who would seek to kill him if they knew that he saw himself as the Messiah and Son of God. Parables gave him a degree of plausible deniability and made it possible for him to teach for longer before the hour of his Passion and death finally arrived.

The Parable of the Sower: Luke 8:4–15

The Word of God is sown on all kinds of soil,
but only those prepared to receive it bear fruit.

Things to Know

- Jesus taught in a straightforward way for the first part of his ministry, but after opposition from his enemies increased, he began teaching primarily in parables.
- Most of Jesus's parables use pastoral imagery that would have been very familiar to his audience, but they can require quite a lot of

information for us to understand in a modern context. Having heard this parable all our lives, for example, we might assume that it was typical for a farmer to sow seeds indiscriminately on obviously bad soil, but this was not the case.

Questions as You Read

Though there are scattered parables mentioned earlier in Jesus's ministry, this parable marked a major shift in the way he taught, moving to parables as a prevailing approach. This time he offered a clear explanation of the parable; still, there's an invitation to meditate more deeply on each type of soil, on the generosity of the sower that borders on imprudence, on what it takes to receive that generosity.

1. What elements of this reading do you find moving? What elements do you find troubling? Confusing? Interesting?

2. The obvious question here is, What type of soil are you? But dive deeper: What are the thorns that choke your spiritual life? Have you, like a path, been so focused on being useful, helpful, and self-sufficient that you've become impermeable to grace?

3. Soil is rich inasmuch as it's empty and broken. What kind of emptiness and brokenness might open you to the Word of God? How can you attempt to let God make you into good soil?

PRAYING WITH THE WORD

What is one word, phrase, or image that spoke to you in your reading? Record it here, and return to it in prayer this week.

The Lost Sheep: Luke 15:1–7

A shepherd leaves his entire flock behind to go off in search of one lost sheep.

Things to Know

- Though we tend to think of this as a parable spoken to sinners about God's desire for their return, Luke tells us that Jesus addressed this parable to the Pharisees and scribes who had complained that Jesus was spending time with public sinners.
- Throughout the Old Testament, God is depicted as the shepherd of his people, Israel, while he also repeatedly chooses literal shepherds to lead his people (Jacob, Moses, David, etc.) to foreshadow his coming as Good Shepherd.

Questions as You Read

This parable is very familiar, eliciting an image of a docile Jesus snuggling a lamb. Is it possible to read it with fresh eyes? Use your imagination, particularly with the strong words used here—words like "desert" and "sets it on his shoulders" and "rejoice."

1. What elements of this reading do you find moving? What elements do you find troubling? Confusing? Interesting?

2. Have you spent time in the desert? What does the image of Jesus going into the desert to seek his sheep evoke that might be

different from the image of Jesus strolling through green, gentle rolling hills? What meaning might this image hold for you?

3. In this parable, the shepherd leaves 99 percent of his sheep at risk of wandering off for love of the 1 percent that he might not even find. What does this recklessness communicate about God's love for his people?

4. This parable reveals that God rejoices when you turn to him. Even when he has to suffer and sweat and search for you, he longs for you and delights in your return. What makes it hard to believe this? If you have one, share a story about experiencing God's mercy.

PRAYING WITH THE WORD

What is one word, phrase, or image that spoke to you in your reading? Record it here, and return to it in prayer this week.

The Lost Coin: Luke 15:8–10

A woman puts all her energy into searching for her lost coin.

Things to Know

- Luke was very concerned with the representation of women in his gospel, frequently pairing stories of men with stories of women.

- Each of the coins in this story was worth an entire day's wage, making her entire savings something like a thousand dollars.

Questions as You Read

This parable may initially be less evocative than the ones that immediately precede and follow it, but consider: This woman had lost 10 percent of her net worth. She wasn't just eager to recover it; she was desperate.

1. What elements of this reading do you find moving? What elements do you find troubling? Confusing? Interesting?

2. What does the image of God being desperate for you do to your heart?

3. This story reveals that God rejoices more over the recovery of the lost than over the continued virtue of the righteous. How do you feel about that truth? Are there certain people or groups of people you struggle to imagine God rejoicing over?

PRAYING WITH THE WORD

What is one word, phrase, or image that spoke to you in your reading? Record it here, and return to it in prayer this week.

The Lost Son: Luke 15:11–32

A father runs to the son who spurned him, eager to welcome him home.

Things to Know

- Asking for an advance on one's inheritance was unusual at best and tremendously shameful at worst. Many commentators believe that this was the social equivalent of the younger son declaring that his father was worth more dead than alive.
- Since pigs were unclean for the Jewish people, there is little that might have been seen as more degrading than spending one's days caring for swine—this is truly rock bottom.
- The robe and ring given to the younger son weren't just festive but indicative of authority. His restoration to a place of honor in the family also likely meant that the older brother's inheritance would be further divided to provide for the younger son at their father's death.

Questions as You Read

Reading this not in a vacuum but as part of this series of parables highlights some of the parallels that Jesus intended us to see. Jesus told the righteous (as well as the lost who were also listening) that sinners are as valuable to God as a lost sheep that he would leave the flock to find, as a treasured lost coin, as half his family. Pay attention to all three of the main characters in this parable.

1. What elements of this reading do you find moving? What elements do you find troubling? Confusing? Interesting?

2. How do you feel about the image of the father running to his son? How might Jesus's listeners have responded to this detail?

3. Compare verse 21 to Pharaoh's confession in Exodus 10:16. Why might Jesus be quoting Pharaoh here? What might he be trying to communicate?

4. This parable reveals that God longs to restore you to relationship with him, no matter what you do. How have you fled from God or squandered the gifts he gives? Describe what it is like to come back to him.

5. Which son do you most identify with? Why?

PRAYING WITH THE WORD

What is one word, phrase, or image that spoke to you in your reading? Record it here, and return to it in prayer this week.

The Good Samaritan: Luke 10:25–37

The enemy of Israel becomes the hero of the story.

Things to Know

- Priests and Levites were the respected religious leaders of Jewish culture; the expectation was that they would be the heroes of a story.

- Samaritans were the neighboring people whom the Jews loathed after many centuries of war between the nations—despite (or, rather, because of) the fact that both peoples were descended from Abraham, Isaac, and Jacob. Even at the time of Jesus, the hostilities continued, with Samaritans having deliberately desecrated the Jerusalem Temple by spreading bones around it only two decades earlier.

Questions as You Read

Though "good Samaritan" has become common parlance for someone selfless, Jesus was subverting his readers' prejudice against Samaritans. He presented two of those who were expected to be righteous and showed them passing by the needy while the enemy of the Jewish people stops to help.

1. What elements of this reading do you find moving? What elements do you find troubling? Confusing? Interesting?

2. Though Jewish tradition insists that the duty to save lives supersedes all ritual norms, the priest and Levite may have refused to help this man for fear that he might turn out to be dead, making them ritually impure by touching a corpse and thus unable to serve in the Temple for a time. Do you ever find yourself in a position where your religious faith or your religious practice gets in the way of your charity? What do you do then?

3. What was the Samaritan risking in helping the man? How might Jesus's listeners have responded when they heard their enemy cast as the one to be imitated?

4. The Church Fathers often write about the Good Samaritan as an allegorical figure representing Jesus. What light does this parable shed on the person of Jesus?

5. This parable clearly asks us to be audaciously generous with those in need, particularly those who can give us nothing in return. What's one practical way you can be generous to someone in need this week?

PRAYING WITH THE WORD

What is one word, phrase, or image that spoke to you in your reading? Record it here, and return to it in prayer this week.

WEEK 9

HEALING MIRACLES

Again we turn to a series of miracles. While our previous section on miracles focused on Jesus's power over nature, this time we'll explore the healing miracles that were the hallmark of his work. Everywhere Jesus went, the sick and the disabled were brought to him with hope that his power would restore them to health and wholeness—and time and again it did just that.

As we study these miracles, we should remember to be astonished by what Jesus was capable of. More than just marveling at his power, though, we should also remember that these miracles were worked not merely as signs to the multitudes but as gifts to individuals—as encounters with God that were intended not just to bring relief to the suffering and communion to the isolated but to bring healing to wounded hearts, conversion to the sinful, and salvation to the lost. Place yourself in the stories as you read and consider what healing and wholeness you might need the Lord to bring to your life.

The Healing of the Hemorrhaging Woman and the Raising of Jairus's Daughter: Mark 5:21–43

Jesus interrupts one miracle to work another.

Things to Know

- More than just being painful and exhausting, the woman's flow of blood made her ritually impure, which meant that she couldn't worship at the Temple and that others couldn't touch her without also becoming impure (Leviticus 15:25–27).
- Luke and Matthew both specify that the woman touched the fringe of Jesus's cloak, a reference to the tassels faithful Israelites were called to wear as a reminder of the commandments of

God (Numbers 15:38–39). The crowds later clamored to touch the fringe of Jesus's cloak, perhaps knowing how it had served the hemorrhaging woman.

- Though the gospels were written in Greek, Jesus speaks to the little girl in Aramaic here. This may indicate that the source of the story (perhaps Peter) remembered the moment so vividly that even if he was recounting it in Greek to a non-Aramaic-speaking audience, he reverted to Aramaic for this one sentence.

Questions as You Read

Each time these two miracles appear in a gospel, the healing of the hemorrhaging woman is sandwiched within the story of the raising of Jairus's daughter, so we can assume that these stories are intended to speak to each other. As you read about the woman's healing, consider the urgency and anxiety of Jairus. As you read about Jairus's faith, consider the faith of the woman who trusted in God despite having been cut off from Temple worship for years because her ailment made her ritually unclean.

1. What elements of this reading do you find moving? What elements do you find troubling? Confusing? Interesting?

2. Considering the controversy that already surrounded Jesus at this point in his ministry, what might Jairus, an official of the synagogue, have risked in seeking his help? What is the cost you face to follow Jesus?

3. Consider the plight of the hemorrhaging woman: physical, social, mental, emotional, spiritual, and financial. What risks did she take by approaching Jesus?

4. As the woman took the time to tell Jesus "the whole truth," how must Jairus have felt? What lesson was Jesus teaching him in stopping not just to heal this marginalized woman but also to listen to her? Why do you think Jesus called the woman "daughter" (the only time in the gospels that he does this)?

5. The mourners ridiculed Jesus for insisting that the girl wasn't dead. What parts of God's promises are difficult for you to believe? How might you learn from Jairus and the hemorrhaging woman?

PRAYING WITH THE WORD

What is one word, phrase, or image that spoke to you in your reading? Record it here, and return to it in prayer this week.

Restoring Sight to Bartimaeus: Mark 10:46–52

Jesus gives sight to a blind man who calls out as he passes by.

Things to Know

- Bartimaeus calls Jesus "Son of David," a messianic title proclaiming him to be the rightful kingly descendant of David and also a way of evoking David's son Solomon, whom Jewish tradition believed to have been a miracle-worker.
- Though previously in Mark Jesus was careful to silence those who proclaimed him and to be circumspect in his healings, here he heals Bartimaeus in the sight of the pilgrim crowds who are traveling to Jerusalem for the Passover.
- In Matthew, Mark, and Luke's gospels, this is Jesus's last miracle before his triumphant entry into Jerusalem on Palm Sunday.

Questions as You Read

Though this story follows the same pattern as many other miracles, where the person in need calls out to Jesus and he offers healing, there's an intensity to Bartimaeus and to the crowd's reaction to him. As you read, imagine the scene: the emotional reactions, the crying and rebuking and springing up. Imagine Jesus's attitude when calling Bartimaeus, when asking what he wanted, when healing him. What is this story telling you about your life?

1. What elements of this reading do you find moving? What elements do you find troubling? Confusing? Interesting?

2. Why do you think the bystanders tried to silence Bartimaeus? What people might feel silenced by our culture? By the Church? By your community?

3. What was it that caused Bartimaeus to keep crying out to Jesus? Have you had a similar experience?

4. When Jesus called him, Bartimaeus "*threw* aside his cloak, *sprang* up, and *came* to Jesus." Despite his blindness, he acted with abandon, even recklessly. What might this teach us about following Jesus?

5. Why do you think Jesus asked Bartimaeus what he wanted when the answer was so obvious? Imagine Jesus asking you this same question: "What do you want me to do for you?" What's your answer?

PRAYING WITH THE WORD

What is one word, phrase, or image that spoke to you in your reading? Record it here, and return to it in prayer this week.

The Raising of Lazarus: John 11:1–44

Jesus seems to ignore his friends' pleas—
and then works an even greater miracle.

Things to Know

- The word often translated as "troubled" in verse 33 is far more forceful than this translation would suggest; the same word is used to describe Herod before he slaughtered the Innocents (Matthew 2:3) and the apostles when they saw a form walking toward them on the water (Matthew 14:26).
- Given how much of the scriptures Jesus's contemporaries had memorized, those who watched Lazarus walk out of his tomb likely remembered the words of Ezekiel: "Then you shall know that I am the LORD, when I open your graves and have you rise from them, O my people!" (Ezekiel 37:13).
- Verse 35 is the shortest verse in the Bible—and one of the most moving.

Questions as You Read

We now encounter Mary, Martha, and Lazarus again, but this time Martha seems to be working very hard to trust God in the midst of far greater pain than that which previously derailed her faith in Jesus's love. Pay attention to the way that Jesus comes to them in their sorrow and the way he grieves, himself.

1. What elements of this reading do you find moving? What elements do you find troubling? Confusing? Interesting?

2. "Now Jesus loved Martha and her sister and Lazarus. ***So*** when he heard that Lazarus was ill, he remained for two days in the place where he was" (John 11:5–6, emphasis mine). Does the conjunction "so" make sense to you here? Can you imagine God's **distance** or

his refusal to answer a need as a product of his love? Have you ever experienced this distance?

3. As before, Martha was honest with Jesus when he came. “Lord, if you had been here, my brother would not have died,” she says, then follows it with a proclamation of faith (that may have taken great effort). When is it difficult to be honest with God in prayer? When you’re upset with the Lord, how can you cling to what you believe? What does prayer look like for you in those times of struggle?

4. Jesus wept over the death of Lazarus and over the grief of those who loved him. Even though he knew he was about to raise Lazarus, he wept. How does it make you feel to consider Jesus’s grief over people’s fleeting sorrow? Can you imagine Jesus weeping with you?

PRAYING WITH THE WORD

What is one word, phrase, or image that spoke to you in your reading? Record it here, and return to it in prayer this week.

WEEK 10

CONTROVERSIES

Our world often dismisses Jesus as a gentle preacher who wandered around telling people to be kind, but men with that sort of mission don't generally end up on a cross. Jesus was gentle—at times—but he was also demanding, preaching truths that infuriated and scandalized his opponents and even sometimes his friends. When we study some of the controversies of the gospels, we're invited to ask ourselves if we're really being faithful to all that Jesus said and taught, or if we're just looking for a God who doesn't threaten our comfortable lives or ask us to love sacrificially.

Forgiving Sins: Mark 2:1–12

Jesus claims the power to forgive sins.

Things to Know

- Though he was originally from Nazareth, Jesus made his home base in Capernaum, a town some twenty-five miles northeast of Nazareth, situated on the Sea of Galilee.
- Jesus frequently refers to himself as the Son of Man, a title that calls to mind a divine figure described by the prophet Daniel (Daniel 7:13–14).
- The scribes were scholars of the law of Moses who drew up contracts and consulted on legal issues professionally; though not all Pharisees, they would have aligned with the Pharisees on most matters and are often depicted as opponents of Jesus.

Questions as You Read

When the paralyzed man's friends ripped the roof off to bring him to Jesus, they were likely only seeking physical healing for him, but Jesus had something else in mind as well. As he offered this gift of mercy, though, he was giving a gift to all those who looked on as well: the revelation that he could forgive their sins.

1. What elements of this reading do you find moving? What elements do you find troubling? Confusing? Interesting?

2. Do you have friends like these, who will rip off the roof to help you? Would any of those friends fight for your holiness in the same way? How can you build up friendships like that?

3. How do you think the man felt when Jesus offered him forgiveness? Have you ever offered a prayer and instead received something else that was good? Were you grateful or resentful (or both)?

4. St. Teresa of Ávila said, "You see, the gift our Lord intends for us may be by far the best, but if it is not what we wanted we are quite capable of flinging it back in his face." How can you receive good things with joy while also honoring your disappointment?

5. Why did some of the scribes accuse Jesus of blasphemy for claiming to forgive sins? What are some other claims Jesus made that people might find shocking? Are any of them hard for *you* to accept?

PRAYING WITH THE WORD

What is one word, phrase, or image that spoke to you in your reading? Record it here, and return to it in prayer this week.

Controversies About the Observance of Sabbath: Mark 2:23–3:6

The sabbath was made for man, not man for the sabbath.

Things to Know

- Every single time Jesus initiated a healing (rather than being asked) it was on the Sabbath, making it clear that his work to reframe the Sabbath was intentional.
- Because failure to observe the Sabbath was understood as one of the reasons for the destruction of Jerusalem in the sixth century BC (Jeremiah 17:27), the concern of Jesus's interlocutors was not unreasonable.
- Pharisees were strict adherents of the law of Moses, while Herodians were supporters of the non-Davidic (and non-Jewish) King Herod, who would have lost little sleep over breaking religious law. Their coalition against Jesus required them to overcome serious differences.

Questions as You Read

It's hard for us to imagine people feeling so strongly about the Sabbath that they conspire to murder someone for his failure to follow it as they expect, but that's exactly what began the efforts of the Pharisees and the Herodians to put Jesus to death. Despite the threat, Jesus continued to work to reframe their understanding of Sabbath—work that was so important to him that he picked this fight again and again.

1. What elements of this reading do you find moving? What elements do you find troubling? Confusing? Interesting?

2. In your understanding, what was the purpose of Sabbath in the Old Covenant? How does Jesus support that purpose by his statement, "The sabbath was made for man, not man for the sabbath"?

3. Given these scriptures, how might you express a Christian approach to Sabbath?

4. What does your Sunday look like? Do you make space for rest and worship on Sundays? How might you be more intentional about the Lord's Day without falling into legalism?

PRAYING WITH THE WORD

What is one word, phrase, or image that spoke to you in your reading? Record it here, and return to it in prayer this week.

Eating with Sinners: Matthew 9:9–13

Jesus calls a public sinner to follow him, then breaks bread with other known sinners.

Things to Know

- When Matthew recounts his conversion, he inserts the story into a series of ten earth-shattering miracles (chapters 8 and 9), showing us that he perceived his call and his conversion as being miraculous.
- Tax collectors in particular were considered not just sinful (a moral judgment) but unclean (a ritual category) because of their close work with non-Jews.
- Sharing a meal with someone was a sign of communion, an indication of unity that symbolized a shared life. For Jesus to share a meal with these people was a very strong statement indeed.

Questions as You Read

Jesus didn't only spend time with those sinners who were ready to turn from sin, but also with those who were still in the midst of their sinful lifestyle—not just former tax collectors and sinners, but current ones as well.

1. What elements of this reading do you find moving? What elements do you find troubling? Confusing? Interesting?

2. Why on earth do you think Matthew left everything behind in response to nothing but the invitation, "Follow me"? When have you had a moment like that with Jesus?

3. Can you imagine Jesus spending time with sinners and enjoying their company? What type of person do you struggle to see Jesus having a good time with?

4. What does it look like to love sinful people the way Jesus did? How can you love people generously and also invite them to holiness?

PRAYING WITH THE WORD

What is one word, phrase, or image that spoke to you in your reading? Record it here, and return to it in prayer this week.

WEEK 11

THE PASSION AND DEATH OF JESUS

This week, we meditate on the darkest moment in human history: when we betrayed the God who loves us, denied him, mocked and scourged him, nailed him to a Cross, and killed him. The gospel writers recount Jesus's suffering and death in detail, dedicating about a third of their gospels to the last week of Jesus's life, with its agony and judgment and crucifixion.

But while it's valuable to meditate on our collectively shared role in the death of Jesus, we have to hold that in tension with his joy in offering himself for us. "For the sake of the joy that lay before him he endured the cross," Hebrews 12:2 tells us. You were that joy. For love of you he died, and for love of you he rose. Blessed be the name of the Lord forever.

The Last Supper: John 13:1–15, Matthew 26:26–30

Jesus washes his followers' feet, then gives them his Body and Blood as food and drink.

Things to Know

- Typically, a slave would wash his master's feet or a woman would wash her husband's feet. This was not a service generally performed by one friend to another, much less a rabbi to his disciples.
- The Last Supper took place at Passover, the holiday that celebrated God's liberation of his people Israel from slavery. At the first Passover, an unblemished lamb was slaughtered at twilight and the people of God were saved from death by being marked with its blood, after which they ate its flesh.

- Just after this reading in John's gospel, Jesus gives his longest discourse in John (John 14–17) in which he gives his disciples his parting words and prays with them.

Questions as You Read

On the night before he suffered, Jesus called together many of his dearest friends—not to console him before his agony, but so that he might strengthen them. In addition to speaking to them and praying with them, he also washed their feet and then gave them his Body and Blood as their food and drink.

1. What elements of this reading do you find moving? What elements do you find troubling? Confusing? Interesting?

2. How would you have felt if Jesus had gotten on the floor to wash your feet? Is it easier for you to serve or to be served? How might this gospel challenge you?

3. Do you feel that the Church has taken this commission to serve others seriously? What do we do well? Where have we fallen short?

4. Think back to our study of the feeding of the five thousand (which also happened during Passover—see John 6:4), where Jesus took bread, blessed it, broke it, and gave it to his followers. How might

that memory of the previous Passover have helped his disciples to understand his actions at the Last Supper?

PRAYING WITH THE WORD

What is one word, phrase, or image that spoke to you in your reading? Record it here, and return to it in prayer this week.

The Agony in the Garden: Mark 14:32–42

Jesus begs the Father to deliver him from his coming anguish but accepts the Father's will either way.

Things to Know

- The Mount of Olives (where the garden of Gethsemane is located) was a location that Jesus frequented when he was in Jerusalem. It's mentioned twice in the Old Testament: once as the spot where the Lord's feet would rest before he fought for Jerusalem (Zechariah 14:4) and once as the place where the weeping King David went in response to the betrayal of a loved one.
- In scripture, a cup is often an image of the wrath of God; see, for example, Isaiah 51:17 and Jeremiah 25:15.
- Peter, James, and John accompany Jesus in this moment; these three appear alone with Jesus at two other times: the raising of Jairus's daughter (Mark 5:35–43) and the Transfiguration (Mark 9:2–8).

Questions as You Read

After giving his Body and Blood to his disciples in the Eucharist, Jesus went out to pray to prepare to give up his Body and Blood on the Cross.

Though he begged his friends to stay awake and pray with him, they fell asleep three separate times, leaving him alone and afraid.

1. What elements of this reading do you find moving? What elements do you find troubling? Confusing? Interesting?

2. What part of this experience do you think was hardest for Jesus?

3. When have you felt abandoned or betrayed? What parts of your experience resonate with what Jesus is going through in the garden?

4. How does Jesus model prayer here? When have you struggled to say, "Not what I will but what you will" and mean it? Is it okay to pray it if you don't mean it?

PRAYING WITH THE WORD

What is one word, phrase, or image that spoke to you in your reading? Record it here, and return to it in prayer this week.

The Death of Jesus: Luke 23:26–49

While we were still sinners Christ died for us (Romans 5:8).

Things to Know

- After the Agony in the Garden, Jesus was betrayed by Judas. He then endured taxing and sometimes violent trials presided over by the Jewish religious authorities (the Sanhedrin), the Judean political authorities (King Herod), and the Roman political authorities (Pontius Pilate) before being sentenced to death, scourged, mocked, stripped, and crucified.
- The account of the Passion is full of prophecies fulfilled, particularly from Psalm 22, Isaiah 53, and Wisdom 2.
- Crucifixion was a tremendously shameful and painful way to die and was thus generally reserved for enemies of the state as a means of discouraging rebellions. One who is crucified dies slowly of a combination of blood loss and asphyxiation.

Questions as You Read

As Christians (and especially as Catholics) we spend much time meditating on Jesus's suffering and death. It's worth praying through each gospel's account, but today we'll look only at Luke, where Jesus's incredible mercy is particularly on display through his last moments.

1. What elements of this reading do you find moving? What elements do you find troubling? Confusing? Interesting?

2. What part of the Passion narrative speaks to you most strongly?

3. Immediately after having nails driven through his hands, Jesus said, "Father, forgive them. They know not what they do." What do you think he meant by "They know not what they do"? What would it take for you to be this generous and merciful? Do you have any strategies that help you to forgive more readily?

4. Why do you think the good thief took Jesus's part?

5. How does it feel to end this session with the death of Christ and not immediately follow it with the Resurrection, as we do whenever we pray the Creed?

PRAYING WITH THE WORD

What is one word, phrase, or image that spoke to you in your reading? Record it here, and return to it in prayer this week.

WEEK 12

THE RESURRECTION OF JESUS

Those of us who have long been Christians and know how Jesus's story ends may struggle to imagine the grief the disciples felt. Jesus had told his friends again and again that he would rise from the dead, but each time they were baffled; it seems they heard in his words not a promise of Easter joy but an assertion of his belief in the afterlife (a disputed position at the time). Most if not all of Jesus's closest friends were convinced that Good Friday was the end of the story, that after the horrors they'd witnessed, nothing could ever give them joy again.

As you read these Resurrection accounts, imagine that you (like they) felt this utter despair with no possibility of future hope. Consider one of the darkest moments in your life, and imagine Jesus redeeming every bit of it, as he did that Easter Sunday two thousand years ago.

The Appearance to Mary Magdalene: John 20:1–18

Jesus appears first to his close friend Mary Magdalene and sends her out to tell others of his rising.

Things to Know

- When John's gospel says "another apostle" or "the apostle whom Jesus loved," tradition holds that this is John's way of referring to himself.
- Though John makes it abundantly clear that he was faster than Peter, he also points out that he deferred to Peter, as head of the Church, and did not go into the tomb until Peter preceded him.
- The garden tomb is reminiscent of the garden of Eden, where Adam was the gardener sent to till the soil. When Jesus calls Mary Magdalene "woman" (the name Eve was called in the garden) and Mary mistakes him for the gardener, we're meant to see the new

creation brought about by the New Adam, Jesus, who has opened paradise where Adam and Eve once closed it.

Questions as You Read

We know little about Mary Magdalene. Jesus cast seven demons out of her (Luke 8:2), and she absolutely refused to leave Jesus. Not when the others ran. Not when he was dying on the Cross. Not when he was dead in the tomb. Mary Magdalene clung to him, and her desperation to be with him ultimately made her the first witness to the Resurrection, which made her the "Apostle to the Apostles."

1. What elements of this reading do you find moving? What elements do you find troubling? Confusing? Interesting?

2. The novelist Graham Greene said of the footrace between John and Peter, "It just seems to me to be first-hand reportage, and I can't help believing it." What details strike you as convincing in this passage? Are there elements that make this Resurrection story harder for you to believe?

3. The text says that John "saw and believed." What exactly do you think he believed?

4. Why do you think Peter and John left after discovering the empty tomb? Why did Mary stay?

5. What do you think it was that blinded Mary to Jesus's identity? What revealed him to her?

6. Have you ever had an experience of resurrection, where God brought peace and joy into a hopeless situation?

PRAYING WITH THE WORD

What is one word, phrase, or image that spoke to you in your reading? Record it here, and return to it in prayer this week.

The Road to Emmaus: Luke 24:13–35

Jesus appears to two companions on the road, but they don't recognize him until he breaks bread with them.

Things to Know

- The disciples had heard the report of the women who had seen an angel announcing the Resurrection, but they dismissed it as "nonsense" (Luke 24:11).
- Cleopas says they were hoping that Jesus would redeem Israel, language that points to the Old Testament concept of a kinsman-redeemer who had the authority to ransom people from slavery (Leviticus 25:47–49), destroy their enemies (Numbers 35:18–21), marry them when they were widowed (Ruth 4:1–12), and bring them home into their ancestral land (Leviticus 25:23–25).

- With its extended scripture study followed by the breaking of the bread, the encounter on the road to Emmaus seems to be the first Mass celebrated after the Resurrection.

Questions as You Read

Cleopas and his companion stayed in Jerusalem through the death of Jesus. They stayed through Easter morning. But when they heard a report of the Resurrection, they got out of town. On the road, they met a stranger who spoke with startling wisdom, but they didn't recognize him until the breaking of the bread.

1. What elements of this reading do you find moving? What elements do you find troubling? Confusing? Interesting?

2. It was only after hearing that the women had seen the risen Jesus that Cleopas and his companion left Jerusalem. Why do you think that was?

3. The two disciples were (it seems) ready to give up on Jesus. Have you ever felt this way? What (if anything) helped you to hang on?

4. Like Mary Magdalene, the two companions didn't recognize the risen Jesus. What might this repeated detail be trying to demonstrate to us?

5. Luke makes it clear that all the scripture study in the world (even conducted by Jesus himself) might not bring a person to faith. Jesus was known to these disciples only in the breaking of the bread. Discuss how scripture has drawn you to Jesus and how the Eucharist has shaped your life.

PRAYING WITH THE WORD

What is one word, phrase, or image that spoke to you in your reading? Record it here, and return to it in prayer this week.

The Appearance in the Upper Room: John 20:19–31

Jesus appears to ten disciples (without Thomas), then waits a week before appearing to Thomas as well.

Things to Know

- The "first day of the week" referenced here is Easter Sunday, the day of Jesus's Resurrection. Jews celebrated the Sabbath on Saturday, the seventh day of the week. With the Resurrection of Jesus, Sunday became the Lord's Day and soon replaced Saturday as the weekly day of rest and prayer for Christians.
- When Jesus gave the apostles the Holy Spirit here, he also gave them the power to absolve sins, a power handed down to all priests.
- Thomas's recognition of Jesus as "my Lord and my God" has become a prayer proclaimed by millions of people around the world at the moment of the elevation of the host and the chalice at Mass, especially in Spanish-speaking communities.

Questions as You Read

After appearing to Mary Magdalene and to two disciples outside his inner circle, Jesus finally came to see the eleven, though without Thomas there. It was a full week before he finally appeared to Thomas as well—a week of doubt and sorrow and confusion for Thomas, and likely anger as well.

1. What elements of this reading do you find moving? What elements do you find troubling? Confusing? Interesting?

2. We imagine that our response to the Resurrection would be pure joy, but for the men who abandoned and denied Jesus it may have been more complicated than that. How might different apostles have felt at Jesus's return?

3. Imagine how you would have felt if you were Thomas and you'd returned to the group to find that Jesus had chosen (presumably deliberately) to come back while you were gone. Would you have doubted? How would you have responded to the other disciples?

4. How might your doubt have developed over the course of the week as your friends maintained their story? What is it like when friends of yours report spiritual experiences or seem to have stronger faith than yours? What keeps you going when you feel distant from God?

PRAYING WITH THE WORD

What is one word, phrase, or image that spoke to you in your reading? Record it here, and return to it in prayer this week.

Final Reflection

Share your experience of this Bible study. How did it compare to your expectations? Do you hope to keep reading scripture in the future? How will you commit to that?

GOING DEEPER

RESOURCES FOR FURTHER STUDY

If this study has lit a fire in you and you'd like to dig deeper into scripture, there are many resources available to you!

- For a heavily footnoted study Bible: *The Ignatius Press Catholic Study Bible*. For a Bible that offers ample room to write notes and observations: *The Ave Catholic Notetaking Bible.* For a Bible with supplemental material that is all written by women: *Living the Word Catholic Women's Bible.*
- For a detailed but easy-to-read exploration of the gospels (with hundreds of references to Old Testament passages to satisfy your curiosity): *Eyes Fixed on Jesus: A Journey into the Gospels* by Meg Hunter-Kilmer.
- For a thorough introduction to the story of Jesus: *To Know Christ Jesus* by Frank Sheed.
- For an overview of salvation history through the whole Bible: *Bible Basics for Catholics* by John Bergsma.
- For academic (but accessible) commentaries on individual books of the Bible: *The Catholic Commentary on Sacred Scripture*.
- For the Old Testament roots of gospel realities, the following books by Brant Pitre:
    - » *The Case for Jesus: The Biblical and Historical Evidence for Christ*
    - » *Jesus the Bridegroom: The Greatest Love Story Ever Told*
    - » *Jesus and the Jewish Roots of the Eucharist: Unlocking the Secrets of the Last Supper*
- For a guided journey through the entire Bible: *A Year in the Word Catholic Bible Journal* by Meg Hunter-Kilmer.

MEG HUNTER-KILMER is a Catholic speaker, author, retreat leader, and campus minister at the University of Notre Dame. She is the author of five books, including *Pray for Us: 75 Saints Who Sinned, Suffered, and Struggled on Their Way to Holiness*; *Saints Around the World*; and *Eyes Fixed on Jesus: A Journey into the Gospels*. She also contributed to the *Living the Word Catholic Women's Bible* and its video series.

Hunter-Kilmer travels the country giving talks on the Catholic faith. She has spoken at the National Eucharistic Congress, the National Catholic Youth Conference, the Columbus Catholic Women's Conference, and more. Her writing has appeared in *Magnificat*, *Our Sunday Visitor*, *Catechetical Review*, and Take Up & Read. She has been featured on various Catholic media platforms, including CatholicTV, SiriusXM's The Catholic Channel, Relevant Radio, and Ave Maria Radio.

Hunter-Kilmer earned her bachelor's and master's degrees in theology from the University of Notre Dame.

She currently resides in South Bend, Indiana.

piercedhands.com
Facebook: @mhunterkilmer
X: @MegHunterKilmer
Instagram: @mhunterkilmer
Pinterest: @ndmeg
YouTube: @ndmeg